W9-CMZ-754

FROM

DATE

GIRLFRIEND CONNECTIONS

Moments of Understanding

GIRLFRIEND CONNECTIONS

Moments of Understanding

by Bonnie Jensen

BARBOUR
PUBLISHING

Illustrated by Julie Sawyer. Designed by Greg Jackson.

Published by Barbour Publishing, Inc., P.O. Box 719, Uhrichsville, Ohio 44683
www.barbourbooks.com

*Our mission is to publish and distribute inspirational products
offering exceptional value and biblical encouragement to the masses.*

 Member of the
Evangelical Christian
Publishers Association

Printed in China.
5 4 3 2 1

Understanding. . .

Girlfriends have a way of knowing how important it is to listen to each other and be there for one another. With little to no explanation, girlfriends are able to discern the need for everything from a hug to a box of chocolates. This little book opens the door to the world of "kindred spirits" that God has deposited in the hearts of true friends. From lightheartedness to sincerity, laughter to tears, girlfriends have a connection not easily broken— a blessing to cherish for life.

$\mathcal{A}$ friend is one who understands where you've been, accepts who you are, sees all you can become, and gently encourages you to grow.

$\mathcal{A}$ friend is, as it were, a second self.

CICERO

Listening is the shortest road to understanding.

How do you know you've found a bosom friend?
She understands what you're saying—
and oftentimes says what you're thinking.

*C*ertain persons do exist with an enormous

capacity for friendship and for taking

delight in other people's lives. . . .

WILLIAM JAMES

Precious, indeed, is the understanding of a friend.

The comfort of a friend is priceless. . . .

Girlfriends are one of God's sweetest gifts.

Friends see the world with a double

perspective but a single heart.

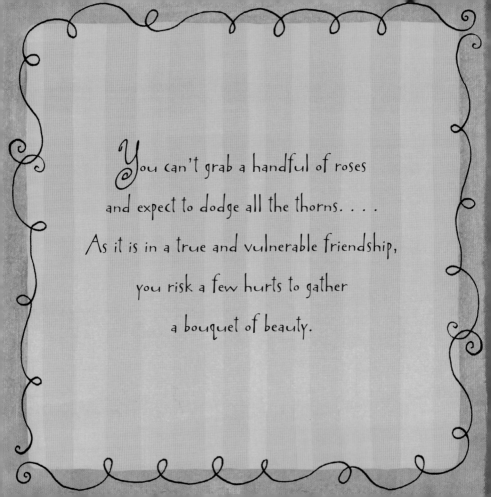

You can't grab a handful of roses
and expect to dodge all the thorns. . . .
As it is in a true and vulnerable friendship,
you risk a few hurts to gather
a bouquet of beauty.

Hold a true friend with both your hands.

NIGERIAN PROVERB

When you find someone who's easy to talk to, treat her with care. . .for God has introduced you to a new friend.

Understanding is one of
friendship's most comforting gifts.

Every good and perfect gift is from above.

JAMES 1:17

Blessed are those who give

without remembering

and receive without forgetting.

UNKNOWN

The glory of friendship is not in the outstretched hand, nor the kindly smile, nor the joy of companionship; it is in the spiritual inspiration that comes to one when he discovers that someone else believes in him and is willing to trust him.

RALPH WALDO EMERSON

*F*riendship is opening your heart

without hesitation. . .speaking your

thoughts without reservation.

$\mathcal{W}$alk beside me,

and just be my friend.

ALBERT CAMUS

Understanding is a fountain of life.

PROVERBS 16:22

Friendship is the inexpressible
comfort of feeling safe with a person,
having neither to weigh thoughts
nor measure words.

GEORGE ELIOT

Let your conversation be always full of grace.

COLOSSIANS 4:6

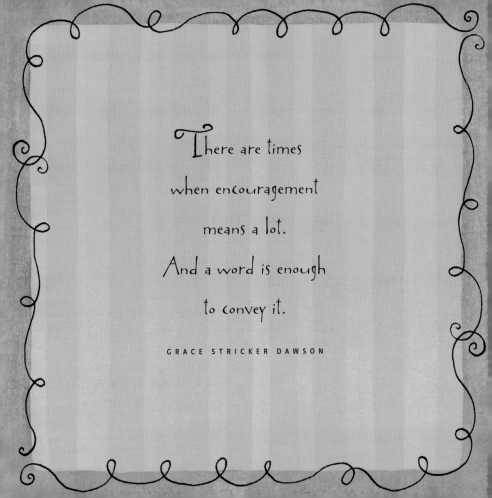

There are times
when encouragement
means a lot.
And a word is enough
to convey it.

GRACE STRICKER DAWSON

There are certain things that
only girlfriends can understand:
the perils of finding the right bathing suit;
chocolate cravings;
skinny vs. "fat" days.

Understood:

Every woman needs a pair of red shoes.

Knowing what to say is wisdom;
knowing what not to say is understanding.

A word spoken in due season, how good is it!

PROVERBS 15:23 KJV

Girlfriends truly see you as you are.
They have a way of reaching beneath the
surface and connecting directly to your heart.

The heart sees better than the eye.

JEWISH PROVERB

Friendship is essentially a partnership.

ARISTOTLE

$\mathcal{A}$s friends, we may look in the same

direction yet see different things;

perhaps it is God's way of helping

us understand another point of view.

True friends wake up in the middle
of the night for a telephone call, drop
everything if they know you're having a crisis,
and send cookies through the mail
if they think it will make you feel better.
Their compassion is priceless—
and so is the fact that we understand
how irreplaceable true friends are.

Good understanding wins favor.

PROVERBS 13:15

It is not part of God's plan that each one of us has beauty or fame. But I believe He did intend for all of us to know the kindness and compassion of a friend.

ANITA WIEGAND

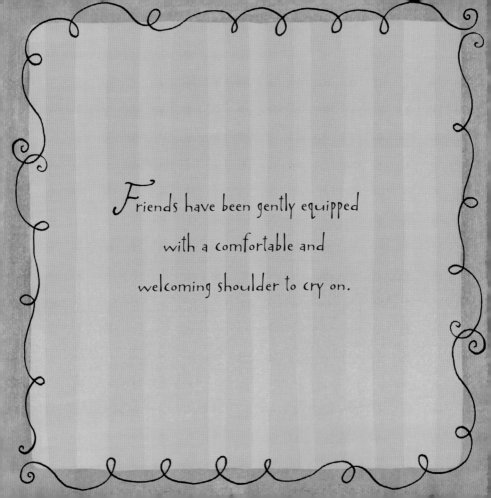

*F*riends have been gently equipped

with a comfortable and

welcoming shoulder to cry on.

Words of despair are slowly eased
as they fall upon the heart of a friend.

Understood:

Sometimes a girl just needs to cry.

When you're not sure what to say,
a hug is a good place to start.

It is easy to discern your closest friends;
they are the ones you run to when you're hurting.

When I was a little girl, I thought it was pretty
important to talk, and I did quite a bit of it.
Then I grew up and discovered
that it's far more important to listen.

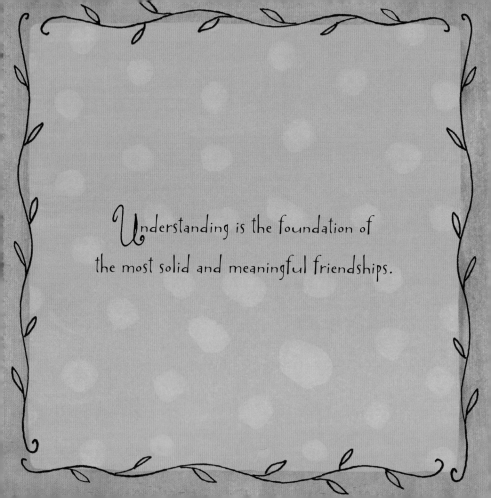

Understanding is the foundation of
the most solid and meaningful friendships.

The road to a friend's house is never long.

DANISH PROVERB

In the presence of a good friend,

even silence is comforting.

It is not so much our friends' help that helps us, as the confident knowledge that they will help us.

EPICURUS

What is a friend?

A single soul in two bodies.

ARISTOTLE

Life is better with friends who care—
always faithful; always there.

Friendship without self-interest

is one of the rare and

beautiful things in life.

JAMES FRANCIS BYRNES

¼ cup of fun + ¼ cup of love

+ ¼ cup of compassion

+ ¼ cup of understanding =

A Girlfriend's Heart!

Through friendship, God has
a vessel in which to pour
His goodness and mercy.

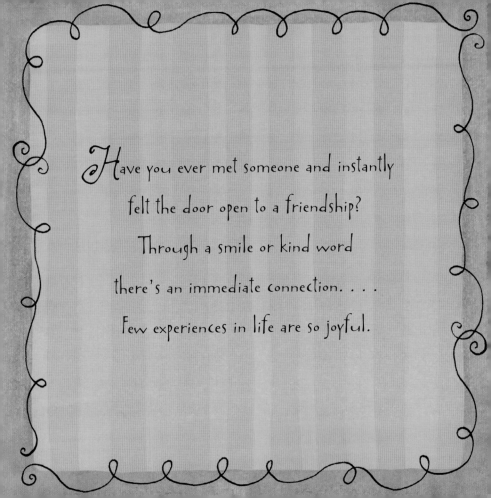

Have you ever met someone and instantly
felt the door open to a friendship?
Through a smile or kind word
there's an immediate connection. . . .
Few experiences in life are so joyful.

Understood:

There is logic in buying something

you don't need just because it's on sale.

God graciously gives us "traveling companions" for the journey of life, and we affectionately refer to them as friends.

How long should we
cherish our girlfriends?
Forever and a day.

$\mathcal{A}$ faithful friend is an image of God.

FRENCH PROVERB

Friends come and friends go,

but a true friend sticks by you like family.

PROVERBS 18:24 MSG

I pray for wisdom to appreciate

the simple things and to understand

the value of making time for my friends.

There was a definite process by which
one made people into friends, and it
involved talking to them and listening
to them for hours at a time.

REBECCA WEST

Do all the good you can.

By all the means you can.

In all the ways you can.

At all the times you can.

To all the people you can.

As long as ever you can.

JOHN WESLEY

God gives us daily opportunities
to express kindnesses to our girlfriends.

I've faced several situations in my life when the encouragement and empathy of friends carried me through. I never ask God why I'm given a trial; I ask Him to help me remember the comfort and understanding I receive from my friends, so that in return, I can offer it to them in their time of need.

God has given each of you some special abilities;

be sure to use them to help each other,

passing on to others God's many kinds of blessings.

1 PETER 4:10 TLB

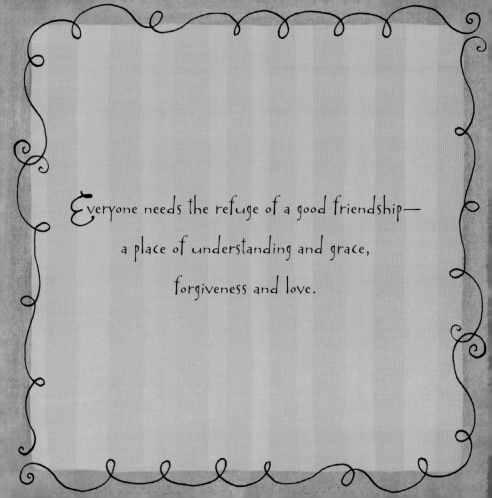

Everyone needs the refuge of a good friendship—

a place of understanding and grace,

forgiveness and love.

$\mathcal{A}$ real friend warms you by her presence, trusts you with her secrets, and remembers you in her prayers.

UNKNOWN

Having a girlfriend to talk to is important; having one who understands you is invaluable.

Understood:

It's perfectly normal to buy a pair of shoes,

even if you have absolutely nothing

in your closet to wear with them.

$\mathcal{A}$ heart in tune with God

is a heart that beats for others.

There are times when two simple words
bring the greatest comfort: "I understand."

Teach us, good Lord,

to serve Thee as Thou deservest:

To give and not to count the cost. . . .

ST. IGNATIUS LOYOLA

Good words to put into practice for a friend:
empathy, helpfulness, warmth, blessing,
thoughtfulness, graciousness, generosity,
kindness, care, consideration. . .

Great is our Lord and mighty in power;

his understanding has no limit.

PSALM 147:5

Having a trustworthy friend is
like having an emergency shelter—
though not in constant use,
there is peace in knowing it's there.

Who understands much, forgives much.

MADAME DE STAEL

*F*orgiveness is a gift we should

readily give to our girlfriends.

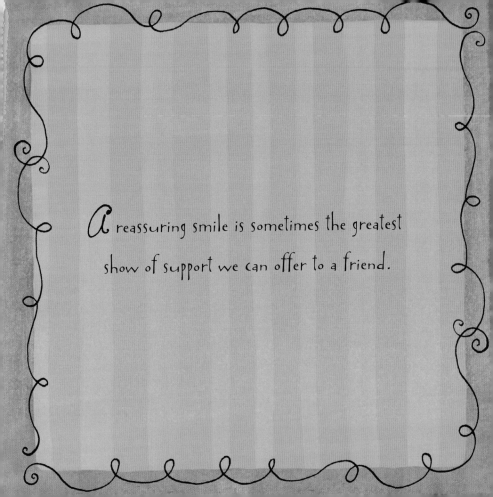

A reassuring smile is sometimes the greatest

show of support we can offer to a friend.

Understood:

Shopping is a woman's version

of the Great American Pastime.

Friendship is where warmth is. . .where love is. . . where memories thrive. A place for comfort, good hugs, and long talks. Friendship is where grace and understanding abide. . . . A place where our hearts always feel at home.

A kindhearted woman gains respect.

PROVERBS 11:16

Message to a Friend

You know so much about giving, yet so little about asking for anything in return. . . . You find a great deal of joy in putting others before you, and none in putting yourself first. . . . You understand weaknesses, appreciate strengths, and empathize with hurting hearts. . . . You are a gift from God.

Good friends, like good books,

are appreciated more fully when

they're not only enjoyed,

but understood.

Friendship is happiness expressed.

God created our hearts with the capacity
and desire for understanding—not only
to be understood, but to understand others.

$\mathcal{E}$very day is a brand-new opportunity

to offer our hands, our hearts, our time,

and our resources to a friend. It is the

giving of ourselves that makes life rich.

Understood:

A woman on the way to the mall

is like the mailman—neither sleet, nor

rain, nor snow will prevent

her from getting there!

$\mathcal{A}$ friendship can weather most things

and thrive in thin soil; but it needs

a little mulch of letters and phone calls

and small, silly presents every so often. . . .

PAM BROWN

Two things girlfriends must be experts in: listening and understanding.

Girlfriends "get" a lot of things no one else does—like the importance of perusing every store before buying. . .the necessity of satisfying a chocolate craving. . .and the essentialness of having at least one pair of jeans that make you look skinny.

One who knows how to show and
to accept kindness will be a friend
better than any possession.

SOPHOCLES

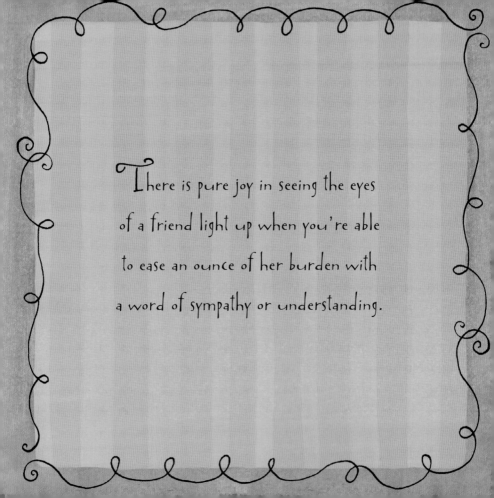

There is pure joy in seeing the eyes
of a friend light up when you're able
to ease an ounce of her burden with
a word of sympathy or understanding.

The LORD gives wisdom, and from his mouth come knowledge and understanding.

PROVERBS 2:6

Every woman needs a girlfriend
with whom to share her innermost
thoughts and deepest feelings.

There's an indescribable feeling inside our hearts when we realize we're truly understood by another person. These are the moments when our friendships are rooted a little deeper and made stronger. It is also a time to thank God—for He is the one who creates hearts so beautifully molded for one another.